# The Power of Purpose

By

Carl F. Hicks, Jr., Ph.D.

and

Natalya H. Bah, PMP, MSPM

ISBN: 1722298634
ISBN-13: 978-1722298630

High Impact Publishing, Chevy Chase, Maryland
www.HighImpactPublishing.com

Printed in the United States of America

# The Power of Purpose

# Table of Contents

# A Note from the Authors

Successful individuals in all walks of life often exhibit similar patterns of thinking and behaving. The authors believe it is helpful for those of you on a success journey to have the opportunity to read about and reflect upon these successful patterns of thinking and behaving that we have observed.

The authors have identified the Success Mindsets as Perspective, Purpose, and Passion and the Success Accelerators as Preparation, Positivity, and Perseverance. Each concise book in the series gives an overview of the topic identified. Additionally, each book provides questions to help you consider and increase your own level of these mindsets and accelerators.

# Introduction

*"There are two great days in a person's life—the day we are born and the day we discover why."*

–William Barclay, Author, Scholar

Knowing your why—your purpose—is a powerful success mindset. Typically, people can tell you what they do for a living, and how they do it, but some struggle with explaining "why" they do what they do for a living.

So why is it important to know your "why," your purpose for doing what you do? Strong determination from the inside enhances what a person is trying to do, be, or become. A clear, internal purpose can channel your energy, provide fuel for your efforts, and keep you focused on your intentions. Once you identify your purpose, you can focus on a more intentional effort toward a goal you want to accomplish. If there's no clear purpose, you may drift off course.

## Purpose transforms activity into achievement.

Purpose is defined as "the reason for which something exists or is done, made, used, etc."[1] Your reason helps you shape your vision and propels you toward your initiative or goal. When you encounter adversity, your reason helps you move forward anyway. People who have a clear grasp of their why—and we equate that with the word "purpose"—can be truly

1. *"Purpose." Learners Dictionary.com 2018. https://www.learnersdictionary.com*

intentional in their efforts. Your purpose comes from your values, beliefs, passions, and what you determine is important to you. It comes from knowing that you have certain talents and from visualizing the results you desire. Once you have taken ownership of your purpose, no one can take it away from you.

With purpose, you can focus more on how you want to live your life—and maybe even how you want to be remembered—as opposed to only what you have accomplished. We all have purpose inside of us, but we have to nurture and shape it. You'll have to surface and enhance your purpose before it can give meaning to your life.

### *Do You Know Where You're Going?*

*Cat: "Where are you going?"*

*Alice: "Which way should I go?"*

*Cat: "That depends on where you are going?"*

*Alice: "I don't know."*

*Cat: "Then it doesn't matter which way you go."*

*-Lewis Carroll, Alice in Wonderland*

*In Lewis Carroll's classic **Alice in Wonderland**, Alice did not have a compelling "purpose" to propel her toward a desirable destination. She may eventually arrive "some place," but is it the "some place" she wanted to be? Or will she just fit herself into the "some place" she has reached?*

*Some people have such a strong purpose that they are motivated to endure all kinds of hardships to reach their desired destination. Their strong purpose provides both a sense of direction and motivation to pursue a specific course of action. They will not settle for less.*

*Others have only a vague notion of what they want or where they are going. They become discouraged at the first obstacle. The lack of a definitive purpose provides little sense of direction and limited motivation. They will likely be tempted to settle for anything.*

# Chapter One

# Discovering Your Why

*"He who has a why to live for can bear almost any how."*

- Friedrich Nietzche, Philosopher

Jeremy Epstein, creator of the blog Never Stop Marketing, and Carl first met in a Starbucks in Washington D.C. a few years ago. Carl was aware of Jeremy's reputation as a forward thinker and as one of the more brilliant minds in marketing. Dan Pink, the noted author of the best-selling books *When, Drive, To Sell is Human*, and *A Whole New Mind,* has said this about him: "Jeremy is one of the savviest marketing minds I've encountered in a long time."

Carl started the conversation, as he does many times, by asking Jeremy, "why do you do what you do?"

Jeremy became so excited about Carl's question that he took out his iPhone, rigged it up on a tripod, and immediately started filming and interviewing Carl about why it was so important to ask *why*. After their time together that day, Carl had a much better understanding of Jeremy's work, and greater insight into the contributions he was making in the world of marketing.

**You will only give your best when you believe
your action has purpose.**

The starting point for your success is knowing your "why." In his book, ***Start With Why***, Simon Sinek draws what he calls the Golden Circle. Envision concentric circles in a bullseye. In the very center of the concentric circles, he places the word "why." He places the word "what" in an outer circle and then places "how" in the outside circle. He says that our belief systems around the worthiness of our activities are reinforced if we can get a solid grasp around why we're going to do something and base it on purpose, intentionality, and values.

Carl's personal Purpose Statement is "to bring out the best in others." As with many of his clients, it took him years to condense his purpose down to that short phrase. One of the main reasons it took him so long was that he kept getting caught up in *what* he did and *how* he did it rather than focusing on the *why*.

A couple of years ago at MIT, Drew Houston,

co-founder of Dropbox, gave the commencement speech and posed this question to the audience: "What is your tennis ball?" He compared a person's purpose to the intentional purpose of a dog chasing a tennis ball.

Visualize a ball flying through the air, hitting the ground, and bouncing around before the dog reaches it. Meanwhile, the dog is racing after that ball. He's going over, around, or through any obstacles to get to the ball. If the ball bounces to the right, the dog pivots to the right. If the ball bounces to the left, the dog pivots to the left.

The dog's purpose is to retrieve the tennis ball and return it to the thrower. It keeps the retriever on an intentional course. Obstacles don't discourage the dog. Instead, the dog seems energized by the opportunity to overcome each and every challenge in its path. To the dog on that day, at that moment, nothing is more important than grabbing that tennis ball and returning it to the person who threw it. We can see the connection to why the dog was chasing the ball—for fun or the excitement of it all—to his purpose, which was to get that ball no matter what!

**Discovering your purpose in life is like finding the missing piece of a puzzle: all the other pieces make sense, and the picture becomes clear.**

One of our favorite questions to ask people, particularly when they are contemplating their own *why*, is "when you're at your best, what are you best at being, doing, or becoming?" When we asked a certified public accountant (CPA) client this question, his answer didn't have anything to do with his being a traditional accountant. Through our discussion, we discovered that his "why" had much more to do with his interest in becoming a lifestyle coach. After our work together, he decided to move in a new direction in order to pursue that why.

Although still a practicing CPA, he is transitioning into a lifestyle coach who works with small, privately-owned, family businesses. This is his true calling. When he allowed his original why to surface, he figured out exactly how he wanted to change his own business to serve a specific type of client. He aligned his purpose with the specific needs of his clients.

**How would you define your *why?***

### The Missing Piece

*"I used to define success as being able to produce*

*any result you wanted, whether it was a*

*relationship, weight-loss, being a millionaire,*

*impacting the culture, changing society,*

*whatever it might be— it might be homelessness,*

*whatever—and lately, I've redefined success as*

*fulfilling your soul's purpose."*

*-Jack Canfield, Author*


*"What is your purpose?" For Jane, the answer to this simple question was one that had always seemed to elude her. She'd been working in marketing for years, and her career was nothing short of impressive, one success after another. She was, for the most part, happy, except for a small,*

*nagging sense that, for all her success, something seemed to be missing.*

*It wasn't until Jane attended her niece's cello recital that she felt something spark to life deep within her. She watched the parade of young musicians that night, each performance a sweet reminder of her own childhood piano recitals. She was struck with the realization that those piano lessons had not only given her a life-long appreciation for music, but had taught her the value of hard work and perseverance, a lesson that had equipped her for her adult success.*

*Upon learning that the music program at her niece's school was in danger of being cut unless independent funding could be found, Jane sprang into action, using her professional skills to organize fundraising efforts. Months later, the program was alive and thriving thanks to Jane's work, and Jane had found a sense of fulfillment and satisfaction in her life that she had never before felt. In helping children have access to music, Jane had found her purpose.*

# Chapter Two

# Clarifying Your Purpose

*"It's never too early or too late to revisit your purpose."*

- Carl F. Hicks, Jr., Author

A few weeks ago, a client Carl was coaching called from Kentucky, where he works as a salesperson.

"Hey, Carl, I've just got to tell you. I visited your website and printed out your 'How to Create a Personal Purpose Statement' worksheet."

He said, "You know, my personal Purpose Statement was once two paragraphs long, and it covered everything. But the sentences I wrote felt cheesy when I said them. I didn't feel good saying them, and it showed."

"So what did you do?" Carl asked.

"In your worksheet, you only have a tiny space where I'm supposed to write my response, and I wrote my purpose in that small space."

"What is it?" Carl inquired.

"I value your values," he responded.

He distilled two paragraphs into a few, simple words, and he now utilizes this sentence as his business tagline.

Clarity of purpose allows you to become more intentional about your why. With clarity of purpose, you don't need two paragraphs to describe your work.

When companies attempt to write a company mission statement, they often write too much, and what they're conveying becomes lost in all the words. When we work with clients, we invite them to refine their ideas and to examine whether they are driven primarily by external measures or by internal beliefs. If their purpose comes from a deeply held belief system, there's a better chance they'll keep going when times are tough.

**Our reasons *why* propel us toward our goal.**

Because purpose is tied into satisfaction and happiness, we recommend that clients write a Personal Purpose Statement. We have a preference for brief statements, because there's power in the brevity. A brief statement invites questions and conversation.

If Carl says, "My purpose is to bring out the best in others," the listener has to follow up with a question like, "Well, how do you do that?" or, "Give me an example of what you do," or, "how does that help a person?"

To help our clients develop a Personal Purpose Statement, we introduce the following thought starters:

**Values:** What do you believe? What do you value? What is important to you?

**Passions**: What do you love to do? What are you passionate about?

**Talents:** What are your super powers? What are you best at doing or being?

**Results:** How do you want to live your life? How do you want to be remembered?

Next, we suggest clients write a phrase or one sentence that incorporates their <u>key values</u>, <u>major passions</u>, <u>outstanding talents</u>, and <u>expected outcomes</u>.

Here's an example of how it can work: let's say Natalya meets someone, and they tell her they're a lawyer. She'll ask for their specialty, and they reply, for instance, that they work in environmental litigation. When she digs deeper to help them uncover their purpose, the lawyer might define this as their purpose: "To ensure that your children don't develop breathing problems because of the pollution in the air."

When they mention Natalya's children, they have her immediate attention. Of course, she will want to know more, so she follows up with a question about how they do that. The speaker has invited Natalya to learn more with their <u>compelling</u>

<u>Purpose Statement</u>.

We have had the good fortune to hear some wonderful Personal Purpose Statements from clients over the years. Here are some examples of concise and compelling statements that illustrate the purpose that drives them:

- Teacher, "To instill in students the joy of learning."

- Teacher, "Broaden the possibility horizons of my students."

- Sales Manager, "Make a difference in the lives of others."

- Chef, "Prepare food that is healthy, tasty, pleasing to the eye, and enjoyable."

- Contractor, "Design and build sustainable and affordable homes."

- Restaurant owner, "Create remarkable and memorable experiences for our customers."

- Software engineer, "Develop software that makes planning for everyday tasks easier."

• CEO/Business Owner, "Change people's lives."

• Financial Planner, "Help people fulfill their financial promises."

**Your purpose reflects your values.**

We invite you to create your own Personal Purpose Statement below that embraces your key values, major passions, outstanding talents, and hint at the expected outcome.

<u>**My Personal Purpose Statement**</u>

### *Be Like the Rain*

*"Act as if what you do makes a difference. It does.'"*
*- William James,*
*American Psychologist, Philosopher*

The rain was falling gently and cooling off the hot, summer day. I was thankful for its presence, and the trees, flowers, and other plants were benefiting from its nourishing effect.

This gentle rain was a giver. It asked nothing in return. Yet, everything growing in the soil would flourish because of its nourishing power.

It made me wonder . . .
- *Do I have a nourishing impact on those I come into contact with?*
- *Do I freely share my gifts to help others flourish?*
- *Do I do so with no expectations of a return?*
- *How can I become like the rain?*
- *How can I provide a gentle, nourishing strength?*

# Chapter Three

# Strengthening Your Purpose

*"If you have a strong purpose in life, you don't have to be pushed. Your passion will drive you there."*

– Roy T. Bennett, Author

Without clarity of purpose, you may not be as intentional about what you're doing, or how you're doing it. Some people, when pursuing an objective, may get discouraged and quit when they reach an obstacle. Our experience with successful people is that they are just as excited about addressing and overcoming an obstacle or problem as they are about achieving their objectives.

They appear to enjoy both the journey and the potential

destination. We've concluded that a clear purpose provides the resolve they need to succeed. But sometimes you have to work hard to ensure your purpose remains the correct one for you to focus on.

In his book *The Power of Why*, Richard Weylman writes that the importance of writing and frequently reviewing our reasons why a particular goal is important cannot be over-emphasized. It's our reasons why that solidify our intentions and purpose. More importantly, our reasons (internal) are much more important to us than reasons given by others (external). Our goals and initiatives are strengthened by our reasons, purpose, intent—and our why!

We encounter a lot of people, especially in bureaucratic organizations, who are going through the motions of living, because they don't have a clear purpose about who they are, what their values are, or what they really want to do. Or they're puruing a career that is separate from their purpose. This almost always results in dissatisfaction on some level in their life.

**Without purpose there is little to motivate effort.**

People sometimes enter careers or professions where they are financially successful, yet they are truly miserable. We've encountered quite a few people who spent time earning advanced degrees and working hard in their profession, yet the answers about their "why" do not reflect their inner purpose.

Once an attorney responded, "I do this because I'm trying to make partner in my law firm, and so I'm working 80 hours a week."

When asked if he loved it, he said no, and that he

barely got to see his family. People like this tell us it's expected of them to work in a certain profession, and they are making a good living (financially), so they continue on that road. They often add that they don't have anything else happening in their life beyond work due to long work days.

It saddens us when people are trapped like that, because it seems that external expectations or extrinsic motivations have robbed them of their true purpose. What happens to that person's legacy if they were to die before they pursued their true purpose? They are successful by those external measures, but they're not truly happy. Yes, they are making a living, but are they making a life?

One benefit of having a crisp purpose is that it is directly tied to happiness. Clarity of purpose goes a long way toward helping you fully understand who you are, what you love to do, what you do well, and how you want to be treated by other people.

If one of these areas is missing in your life, your happiness will suffer. If one of these areas goes unfulfilled for long periods of time, you may feel as though you have a "hole in your soul." Sometimes we must revisit our purpose to determine if we need to make an adjustment—like the accountant client did. Some of us have the ability to refine and sharpen our purpose as we gain experience in our profession or occupation.

It is helpful to remember that our purpose needs intention as well as attention in order to strengthen it. People with a strong purpose tend to be the most successful, because they keep moving forward no matter the obstacles. Just as muscles atrophy because of lack of exercise, our purpose can also weaken if we don't do the things that strengthen it.

How often do you "feed" and reaffirm your purpose? How frequently do you express your gratitude for the assistance that others have given you as you pursue your purpose? How often do you revisit your Personal Purpose Statement? How often do you learn something new in order to firm up your purpose?

When we have internal strength and purpose, that's power. The power of purpose brings clarity to the reasons you want to do something, which is linked to your belief systems and values. Outwardly, that turns into your drive, goals, focus, and intentionality.

Goals mean absolutely nothing if they are not
connected in some meaningful way to your
values and what's important to you.
What values are behind your purpose?

### Commencement

*"With the new day comes new strength and new thoughts."'*

*- Eleanor Roosevelt, Former First Lady, Diplomat*

*I always enjoy watching the conclusion of a graduation commencement service when the graduates toss their caps into the air. You can almost hear a collective sigh of relief. "Now, finally, this experience is over. We made it through those four years!"*

*Yet, for those of us who have been through a commencement celebration, we know that it is just the beginning. Hopefully the past four years have equipped us with the ability to learn on our own for the rest of our lives.*

*In a sense, each day is a commencement, a beginning. What will each of us choose to do with a new beginning? What opportunities will open up to us because we are alert to them?*

*Will we have the opportunity to bring happiness into the life of someone who very much needs kindness? Will we embrace the challenge of learning something new that might come in handy in the future? Will we progress further on our Greatness Journey, enjoying each step of the way?*

*Congratulations! You have now graduated into the future!*

# Conclusion

*"Effort and courage are not enough without purpose and direction."*

– John F. Kennedy, 35th U.S. President

In this book, we have stressed the importance of having a purpose—a vision for what you want to accomplish. You can make a direct connection between having a defined purpose and your happiness and success. Living your life and making decisions based on a well thought-out purpose is the optimal way to proceed. You've seen a direct connection between not pursuing your purpose and experiencing deep dissatisfaction.

One message from this book is the importance of

having a process to determine your purpose. The first step is defining your why—why you do what you do. It's important that you ask *why*, and that you separate your *why* from your *what* and *how*.

The benefits of drafting a Personal Purpose Statement were also discussed, which results in a concise definition of what drives you. By writing down your purpose, you are in a better position to align your life with it. But, just defining your purpose is not enough. You need to revisit your purpose often to ensure it is still relevant for you at each stage of your life. Periodically, you will want to strengthen your purpose. The stronger your purpose, the more likely you'll be able to stay true to what you're trying to achieve.

A strong purpose is like a magnet. Instead of metal objects, it's your key values, major passions, outstanding talents, and expected outcomes that are attracted to it. The stronger the magnet, the stronger the attraction, and the more likely these items will be aligned.

And remember, you can also use magnets to help determine your direction. Your purpose helps you navigate the right direction for your life.

**What future do you dream of for yourself?**
**How would it feel to achieve it?**

## *Sting of Days*

*Each day is a mini lifetime.*

*When you wake up in the morning, do you ever think that it is the first day of the rest of your life?*

*And when you go to bed at night, do you reflect back on the day and realize that it is gone forever?*

*Did you make the day what you wanted it to be? What was your legacy for that day?*

*Life is a string of days—a series of mini-lifetimes. Each day brings with it a new beginning and ends with a legacy of some kind.*

*Are you beginning each day with the determination to make it great? Are you ending each day satisfied with its results?*

*You can only live one day at a time; live each with purpose.*

# The Power of Purpose

# About the Authors

Carl F. Hicks, Jr., consults with successful senior executives and business owners who want more. More personal and professional growth. More productivity and profitability. More meaning and happiness. More quality thinking time.

As President/CEO of The Growth Group, LLC, Carl works with some of America's best-managed companies helping them to identify and develop their top managerial talent, strengthen their work teams, and optimize their organization's performance.

Through his conversational-coaching approach, Carl keeps clients actively engaged and focused on critical strategic initiatives, growth, and profitability - while maintaining a balance between their Life Style Goals, their Livelihood Goals, and their Quarterly Strategic Initiatives.

Clients range from emerging entrepreneurs to Fortune 100 firms. His results-oriented approach to management combines a formal education—Ph.D. in Business Administration and MBA from The University of Arkansas and B.S. in Management with Distinction from Mississippi State University — with more than thirty years of practical consulting experience.

Carl is on the Board of Directors of Lifetime Financial Growth, LLC, and has been recognized by Birkman International as a Birkman Master Certified Professional, a designation earned by only 5% of their consultants worldwide. Carl is also an **active member of Forbes Coaches Council**.

Carl and his wife, Carolyn, have a daughter, Natalya, and son-in-law, Mahmoud, who have blessed them with three wonderful grandchildren. Carl and Carolyn share their homes in Chevy Chase, Maryland, and Hilton Head Island, South Carolina, with Delta, their beloved Maltese.

Natalya H. Bah helps individuals and organizations alike define and achieve their goals. With services such as team building, executive coaching, and in-person and online training, she caters to a wide variety of interests and needs. The clients of Natalya H. Bah Consulting come from many fields ranging from legal, financial services, and real estate, to government and non-profit.

As a certified Birkman Method© consultant, Natalya utilizes the highly effective self-assessment program, along with other activities and exercises, to foster team building and strengthening in her clients. Past sessions have specifically focused on increasing effective communication, preparing for organizational change, increasing employee engagement, and understanding and meeting motivational drivers.

For her executive coaching services, Natalya created the Define and Achieve Your Goals Process™, which includes companion workbooks and online courses such as "Getting Goal Ready." This process is available for both individuals and groups.

In addition to the courses she offers online, Natalya creates and delivers in-person training on project management and leadership. She has used her training services to help organizations develop leaders, improve their project success rate, and meet their strategic goals.

Natalya has spoken at a variety of conferences and symposiums. With a relaxed, interactive facilitation style, she speaks to groups of all sizes on a wide range of topics including goal-setting and achievement, project management, self-assessments, employee engagement, and change management.

Having received her Master of Science degree in Project Management from George Washington University's School of Business, Natalya is also a certified Project Management Professional (PMP). She lives in Bethesda, Maryland, with her husband, Mahmoud, and their three children.

## Also Available by Carl F. Hicks, Jr.
## and
## Natalya H. Bah

### *The Power of Perspective*

By

Carl F. Hicks, Jr.

and

Natalya H. Bah

Are you living the life you want to live? A life of purpose? Of meaning? Are you on your way to reaching the level of success you believe you're capable of? If not, it's time to harness the Power of Perspective.

Available now at Amazon.com

## Also Available by Carl F. Hicks, Jr.

The Best You

Inspirational Quotes to Grow Your Best Self

By
Carl F. Hicks, Jr.

### *The Best You*

By

Carl F. Hicks, Jr.

A collection of motivational quotes by Carl to help spark a thoughtful assessment of where you are now, and inspire a vision of where you'd like to go.

Available now at Amazon.com

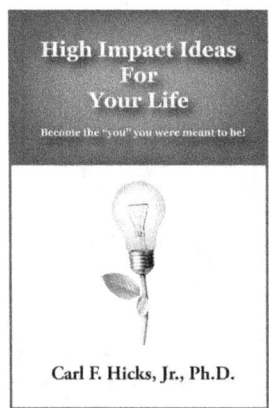

*High Impact Ideas for Your Life*

By

Carl F. Hicks, Jr.

Are you living the life you love and loving the life you live?

In this collection of thoughts and observations be inspired to rekindle your dreams, embrace your potential, and achieve what is possible in your life. Learn how to enjoy the life you were destined to live!

Available now at Amazon.com and
Barnes&Noble.com

*Unlock the Growth Potential of Your Organization*
By
Carl F. Hicks, Jr., Ph.D. and
Martin E. Willoughby, Jr., J.D.

With this innovative tool, learn how to understand and motivate each individual in your organization in order to achieve collective success.

Available now at Amazon.com and
Barnes&Noble.com

# Are you ready for a Hicks Fix?

## Visit **TheHicksFix.com** today!

Learn more about The Growth Group, LLC, awareness and growth enhancing services:

- Executive Coaching
- Team Strengthening
- Organizational Optimization

Discover valuable resources:

- Monthly High Impact Ideas and Coaching Tips
- Podcasts
- Worksheets
- Videos

THE GROWTH GROUP
Consultants to Management

**Read on for excerpts from the**

**Power Series:**


The Power of Perspective


The Power of Passion


The Power of Preparation


The Power of Positivity


The Power of Perseverance

# The Power of Perspective

By

Carl F. Hicks, Jr., Ph.D.

and

Natalya H. Bah, PMP, MSPM

## *Excerpt*

# The Power of Perspective

*"A change in your perspective can result in a seismic shift in your life."*

–Natalya H. Bah, Co-Author

Art loved the view from his second story balcony. From that perch, he could enjoy the daily sunsets over the Pacific Ocean. He found the fading colors invigorating. His colleague Dave, on the other hand, could never see nor appreciate the sunset from his basement apartment.

Sometimes Art and Dave would have the opportunity to work together on the same project. Both were equally skilled and talented and had graduated from top universities. Yet Art and Dave's perspectives of what was possible were as different as their views from their apartments. Art had an expanding perspective and was never deterred when issues or obstacles arose. Dave, on the other hand, had a confining perspective. Dave would get frustrated by unexpected changes and saw them as barriers, not opportunities to do things better.

Art's perspective on life tended to reflect his "balcony" view. With that perspective, Art continued to grow and develop and eventually moved into his dream job. His career advancement was enhanced by his "balcony" view.

Our perspective determines how successful we'll be in our work and life. It influences how we think and see the world and how we interact with people and react to events. Successful individuals have a perspective that tends to drive them toward successful outcomes. They tend to see opportunities in problems. They look on the bright side of things and visualize results.

As you read this book, we invite you to examine and reflect upon your perspective. When was the last time that you really considered what your perspective was, and how it might be affecting your life? How does your perspective affect how you see and react to situations in your life and career? How in control of your perspective are you?

Perspective is a powerful word. It's defined by Merriam Webster as providing "the ability to understand what is important and what isn't."[1] Would you benefit from the

1. "Perspective." Merriam-Webster.com 2018.https://www.Merriam-Webster.com
(7 March 2018)

opportunity to consider what is important in your life, and how you can harness this powerful tool to make you more succussful?

Throughout this book, we will provide you with questions that will help you investigate and strengthen your perspective. We hope you'll allow your perspective—hopefully from the balcony and not the basement—to drive you toward personal and professional success.

***A Moment of Perspective . . .***

***How is your vision?***

Some people view the world through the lens of rose-colored glasses. Others see the world through "woe-shaded" glasses.

But there are some who choose to wear "vision" glasses and "see" what's not there . . . but could be.

· They see an opportunity, where others

 may see a problem.

· They see a future, where others may

 be stuck in the past.

· They envision greatness, while others

 experience envy or fear.

So, how is your vision? Is it time for an eye exam?

# The Power of Passion

By

Carl F. Hicks, Jr., Ph.D.

and

Natalya H. Bah, PMP, MSPM

*Excerpt*

# The Power of Passion

*"Working hard for something we don't care about is called stress.*
*Working hard for something we love is called passion"*

–Simon Sinek
Author, Motivational Speaker

Passion is a powerful force. It is the major fuel for achieving our dreams and our goals. What is your passion? When was the last time you took inventory of your passions and considered whether you are living your life pursuing them?

Passion is defined as a "strong liking or desire for or a devotion to some activity, object, or concept."[1] The more passionate we are about something, the more likely that we

1. *"Passion." Merriam-Webster.com 2018.https://www.Merriam-Webster.com*
*(7 March 2018)*

will be successful at it. Think about people you've known who have been very passionate about their work. Doesn't it seem like those are the ones who receive the greatest notice and accolades? They live their devotion and are rewarded for it.

Sometimes we get stuck at a place in our life's journey, and we need help in getting unstuck. It may be helpful to refine, clarify, and crystalize what we are truly passionate about. We cannot overemphasize the power of passion as a propellant to helping us fulfill our dreams.

This book will walk you through rediscovering your passion by providing questions to help you think deeply about your passions. We'll then clarify your passions by revisiting activities you greatly enjoyed as a child and how to use other factors to more deeply understand your passions.

Finally, we'll discuss why pursuing your passion is

important to becoming the "you" you were meant to be.

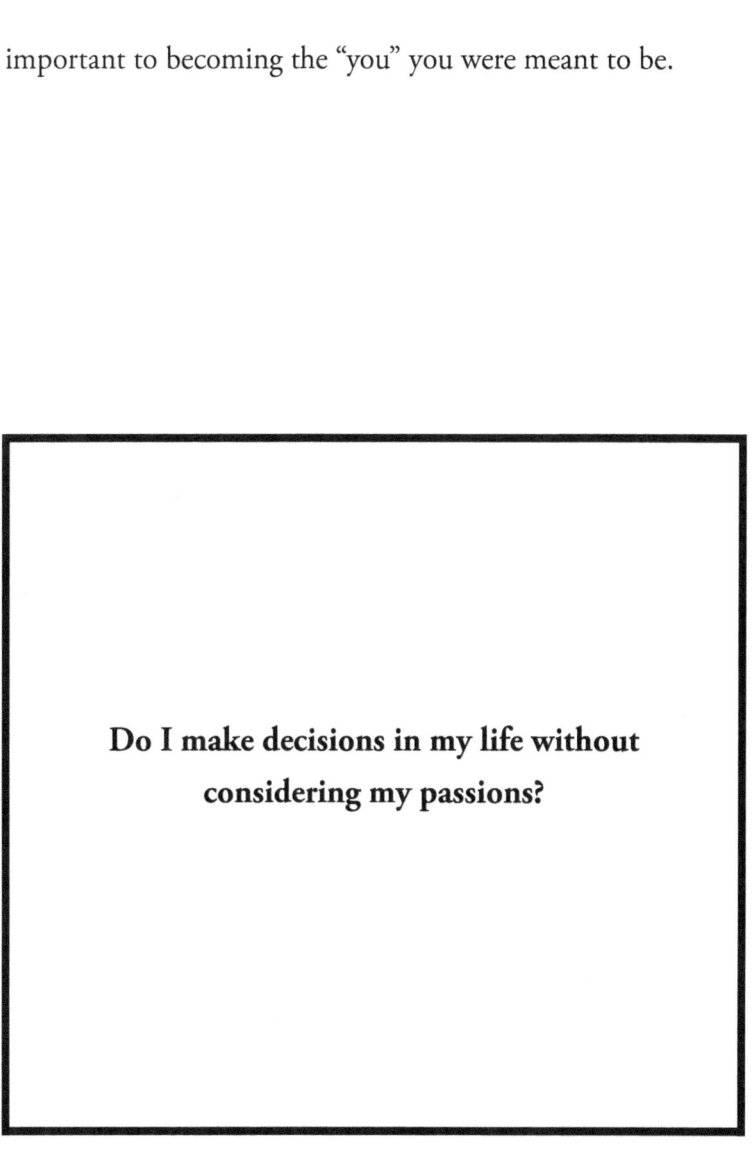

**Do I make decisions in my life without considering my passions?**

# The Power of Preparation

By

Carl F. Hicks, Jr., Ph.D.

and

Natalya H. Bah, PMP, MSPM

## *Excerpt*

# The Power of Preparation

*"There are other players who were more talented, but there is no one who could out-prepare me."*

–Peyton Manning
Two-Time Super Bowl Champion
Five -Time National Football League Most Valuable Player

***Semper Paratus –United States Coast Guard Motto***

Continuous preparation is a hallmark of champions, and a strong perspective can be enhanced by intentional, purposeful, determined, definitive, and disciplined preparation. Being fully prepared occurs one step at a time, and preparation can be conceptualized as the build-up of useful skill sets over time.

Each of us needs to ask ourselves, "What skills do I need to ensure success?" and "What do I need to know how to do exceedingly well to be *Semper Paratus*—always ready?"

Intentional and purposeful preparation suggests that one devote considerable thought to the *why* and *what* of the planned preparation. Are you wanting to improve an already established skill? Do you want to strengthen a skill that has the potential for further development? The most likely response will be a "yes" to both questions.

Peyton Manning spent countless hours reviewing game film, notes by scouts, and his own thoughts in preparation for each game. He once said that he may not have been the most skilled player on the field, but he was the most prepared. A blog post by Sport Psychology Quotes (July 21, 2011) quoted Manning describing his consistent preparation:

> "In the NFL game today, there are a lot of better athletes than I am, and quarterbacks these days are faster than the quarterbacks have always been,

they're running like crazy. But I kind of stick to my roots of the disciplined quarterback. You know, I'm doing the same routine every week, studying tapes and working hard, getting ready to play and making good decisions on Sunday."

The thoroughness of Manning's preparation manifested itself in wins, MVP awards, and a number of other individual and team NFL records. In his final game as a professional football player, his team won the 2016 Super Bowl. Peyton credited his intense preparation as a contributing factor to his confidence.

Dr. Denton Cooley, the noted heart surgeon, completed the first successful heart transplant in the United States and performed more than 120,000 open heart operations during his career. He had great manual dexterity and surgical efficiency. Other surgeons commented on his lightning speed, the huge volume of daily surgeries, and his "Tiffany-level" quality. Surgeons came to Houston from all over the world to observe his procedures.

Dr. Christian Barnard said, "It was the most beautiful surgery I had ever seen. No one could equal it. Dr. Cooley's skill was matched by his grace and kindness."

His surgical procedures were focused, decisive, efficient, and effective—all outcomes of his intentional and purposeful preparation. One example of his purposeful practice involved tying knots inside of a small box as preparation for efficiently tying off surgical sutures in the confined space of a patient's chest cavity.

Champions such as Peyton Manning and Dr. Denton Cooley were able to reach the highest levels of achievement in their respective fields through dedication, hard work, and purposeful preparation. They were fortunate to have been in a calling where what they loved to do and what they did well came together.

Some may say that they were lucky. Luck may play a role, but their success did not happen by chance. Their 'luck' was the result of their preparation meeting with opportunities presented to them. "Luck is what happens when preparation meets opportunity," claimed Seneca.

The question of what to prepare for finds its response in the clarity of one's perspective. Preparation is enhanced by the clarity of your perspective. As you gain clarity about how you see the world, what you want from it, and what you are willing to do to get what you want, the preparation necessary becomes clear.

# The Power of Positivity

By

Carl F. Hicks, Jr., Ph.D.

and

Natalya H. Bah, PMP, MSPM

*Excerpt*

# The Power of Positivity

*"If you think you can do a thing or think you can't do a thing, you're right."*

–Henry Ford
Founder of Ford Motor Company

If you think you can change your way of living by changing your way of thinking, and you take action, then we believe you can.  However, if you think that you can't change your life for the better, and you don't even try, then you won't. How we see a situation or an event or respond to people's words depends upon how we think about where we are, who we are, and what we can do. In short, how we *think* influences our lives and actions.

### *"I can do this!"*

Several years ago, when one of our granddaughters was about six years old, my wife and I (Carl) took her to a birthday party at a bowling alley. I hadn't been in a bowling alley in a long time and I wondered, "How are these children going to be able to lift the bowling ball and throw it down the lane?"

What I found out was that the alley adds a bumper for children to prevent gutter balls. If the child can toss or drop the bowling ball, it'll roll down the alley. With the bumper, it'll continue down the lane and most likely hit some pins.

Two children, in particular, caught my attention with their different approaches to the game. The first was a three-foot girl who weighed about 30 pounds. Each time it was her turn, she'd become excited, jump around, and say, "I can do this. I can do this. I can do this."

She'd grab a bowling ball and struggle up to the line and drop the ball. She obviously couldn't throw it, because it was too heavy. Although she could barely make it up to the line, she'd drop the ball and then start jumping and yelling, "Strike! Strike! Strike!"

The ball rolled slowly, yet it would knock some pins down with the assistance of the bumpers. I noticed that she actually made two strikes. It was always exciting to watch her jump up and down and yell, "Strike! Strike! Strike!" every time she bowled.

In contrast, a four-foot boy weighing about 15-20 pounds more than the girl would complain about the weight of the ball and how hard it was to bowl. His hunched shoulders revealed his reluctance as he walked up to the line. He was bigger and had more strength than the girl, so he should have been able to put more force behind the ball before throwing it down the alley. After he threw the ball, however, I noticed he would turn to his left and walk away with his head down and a dejected look on his face. He would say, "This is too difficult. The ball is too heavy, and the pins are too far away."

Almost every time, the ball would move to the left and ride down the bumper. It would hit just one or two pins. I never saw him get a strike.

**Locus of Control**

As I watched these two children bowl, it dawned on me that the young girl who was approaching this activity in a positive manner had what we call an internal locus of control.

Locus is another word for location. People who have an internal locus of control about a certain event or activity in their life believe that they can exert some impact on the result that might occur. Her jumping up and down and yelling, "Strike! Strike! Strike!" indicated that she believed that she could do it, and on a couple of occasions she actually did.

The opposite of internal locus of control is what's referred to as an external locus of control. This refers to a belief that one can't change an outcome no matter what actions are taken, and that one's results are beyond one's control.

Our loci of control varies depending upon the situation or task. For example, the very next day the young man may have had an internal locus of control as he was out on the soccer field, and the young woman may have had an external locus of control as she was at art class. We're always somewhere on that continuum.

# The Power of Perseverance

By

Carl F. Hicks, Jr., Ph.D.

and

Natalya H. Bah, PMP, MSPM

## *Excerpt*

# The Power of Perseverance

*"On the steep slope of success can be found the victorious who are determined to persevere and to reach their dreams."*

–Carl F. Hicks, Jr., Co-Author

After eighteen years of trying, Sergio Garcia won the Masters on Sunday, April 9, 2017, in his 74th attempt at winning a major golf title. He began his journey in 1999 when he first captivated golf fans at the PGA Championship. Over the years, he encountered one disappointment after another with losses and close wins. Garcia persevered through hardships and frustration and teaches us all to never give up. He's considered a true champion—not just because he won— but because he never gave up on his dream.

Success stories have three major parts: the beginning, middle, and end. In measuring success, we often focus on the difference between the start of our success journey and the completion or results achieved. The middle part, the route between start and finish, can contain ups and downs, starts and stops, and zigs and zags. It's rarely a straight line. The middle part of success can be a mixed bag.

It's in this middle part when you may start to experience obstacles. Situations can become complex and people frustrating. Sometimes, it may seem that the harder you work, the further behind you get, or you may feel trapped by circumstances beyond your control. Negative emotions can start to dominate your thinking and affect your behavior. You may entertain the idea of quitting.

It is precisely at this time that you will

need to dig deep inside of yourself and pull up all of your perseverance reserves.

I like to define perseverance as the ability to steadfastly stay the course in the pursuit of a goal, task, dream or journey, regardless of the difficulties, distractions, or obstacles faced, or the frustration and discouragement experienced. What do you think of when you hear the word perseverance? When was the last time to considered how your ability to persevere impacts your life?